THE DIS / SONANCE

Columbus, Ohio
empbooks.com

First Edition:10 19 33 34 6 11 1973
ISBN: 979-8-88596-191-2
LOC: 2023947266

Creation, Design, and Layout: Kym Cunningham
Approval Masquerading as Editing: Ezhno Martín
Author Photo Credit: Vinh;Paul Ha
Cover:Rebecca Cunningham

THE DIS█████████

[IM WE]

RECOGNIZES

█████████SONANCE

[IM YOU]

ACKNOWLEDGMENTS

This collection is indebted to the emotional, intellectual, and spiritual labor of many writers, both those with whom I have worked intimately and those whom I know only through intimacy with their work (for more complete reference, please see MANUAL).

As for those who I have the privilege to know, I am tempted to leave you without names—maybe it's safer that way. In the not-naming, I don't risk further, meaning there is something possible.

But the reality is that you know who you are. Which is to say I have been molded and shaped—in irreconcilable ways—by these intimacies: every conversation, every critique, every suggestion for further inquiry.

This is what leaks from these pages—the energy you have given. I hope you find what is proffered as nourishing as I have. Thank you.

WHAT CONTENTS

PART ONE

& WHITENESS THREATENS CHOKE

when i say sugar   im not calling you   honey
i mean   theres no poison   in the afterbite
to your tongue   something   allergic
causing a swell   shut   your mouth
i shouldnt   make skin   digestible
but could eat   if i wanted
swallowhole   clouding
your body   with mine
crystallized&   communicable   for a beloved
was i always parasite   were you perishable
who clings   &refuses   to let go
sucking shade   from flesh
to turn you   sticky   a sheen
or chemical   hint
weve forgotten   what sweetness   tastes like
something expected
you cake   to my lips
& mix with milk   in the smother   what falls
from the sky   sticks
to your ribs   like how   a hand dissolves
ridges   as unpreserved
narrative
in exfoliation
or
what   hasnt been   said
we are only
a series of breaths

EX LINGUA JUS ORITUR

what happens is i watch
a question of gnawing &
picking teeth with your bones
or was it to deter
like when we gave
more than could be chewed
your skull might smile at
my foot stuck
inside the inside
breaking open your ribs
give me as a gift
& we know
through
congress in the way of the beast
beware
carnal urges
that which demands
in place of the mother tongue

as the law eats your body not
spitting you out but
a familial cliche as raison detre
that social entree
orders appetite bit off
if only we swallowed
how a phrase turns
in the knot of your back
we flay what we sew
to write covenant on your heart
slick as hairs breadth
the path out of harm is
an ouroboros of white dog
means no one is safe from himself
a vicious circling of
beginning
as father gaps
between the teeth

PERSON

as in

per our

sons request

to be

used

not born

in a sentence

we await

the absorb

but was it his

or ours

what screams

through the placenta

some poetry

better to remain

unmade

being cleansed of skin

is a book our body

not named

but eaten

what we ll pass as one

propositions

over & onto

the other

for inheritance

of what is expelled

THE DEAD MATTER

itwasntsomuch theywereabsence butsmoke whathappens intheafter &lingers

howshecouldsee butnotfeel thegulfbehind easytomistakeliving foralive adangerof

theunburied shewantedthem toteachher howblood movesbetweenworlds howto

distinguish mythfrombeliefinthe alchemyofmarrow& whetherthedifference between

revenants &gods wasamatterofworship howtheystuck totheteeth likeflesh ormoved

likeaspine

theyknew whatitmeant tocreatesomething fromnothing notmissed butbreath

theyappeared oppositeofefficiency excess takingupspace astorywithinastory trapped

inbody whorests &whatveilsuncover orcloak thevaporswe cannotpasson but

survive howwe share intheremains

butshefoundinheritance boundtotheroot wonderinghowto brandahaint whatsound

the searmakes &whetheritsmells likefires memory couldsheeatit whatmightthey

taste condemnedastheywere torend&swallow shroudsoftongues sotheirmessage

stayed unspoken

wewhohave smallthroats butcavernousstomachs whatdecays ormustbecontained
howthedesert erasesthebody madeofthirst sheofhunger &howthesewere thesame
adesireto touch&betouched abodyforgetting whatitlikes& whatwe holdforransom
adepartedcurse oflead&salt whatcan notbereclaimed

isthisdissolving howweslip beneaththesurface likesugarinwater whichistosay notat
all & how stillnessresuscitates whatisexchanged takingusbeyondourselves when
spectral foretellshow wefade intowhitespace whatcanbestolen &speculatedmeans
weaskthattheend beapocryphal& whatiserased

SHE READ GOD

LED SHE GOD

SHE GOD READ

SHE LEAD GOD

SHE READ GOD LEAD

DEAD**GODSHEREAD**

SHE

BUT THEN WHAT WREAKS

SHE　　RED　　GOD　　　　　　　　　　　　　LEAD　　SHE　　GOD

SHE　GOD　LED　　　　　　　　　　GOD　SHE　RED

SHE　LED　GOD　RED

LEADSHEGODBLED

HE

ROOTS　&　LEAVES

PUNC TU ATE DARC HIVE

it is said skin   is allegory   for the aesthetics

           of sur   face   i stand   transfixed by

an ellipsis   of moles   under your eye

           what thought   a body couldnt finish   the period

against my mouth   silencing   the gods   if

only i believed   the commas   a round   my brow   paused

           pre   speech   how a glance   can die   waiting

maybe mention   the parenthesis   before your lips   out of

           context   what ill   never   say

           as you remain   an unsaid

argument   asks is discourse   pronounced   by how

           weve been   raised   neither being

           grammatically correct   but fitting   a word inside

a word inside   the skin   to peel back

           s m o t her   vessels anticipating   fulfil

lament with   interlocutors cheeks   of honey&mud   what we

           spread   between your risk&my   habeas corpus

as in you   should have   writ of   the body

           the work   dispossessed   so

10

tell me   a story   i want you   r   indices of home
                        signed&signified   et my elegy
        the difference   between death   & dying lying
                        inpotent extinction   we should not   defame
by naming   palimpsest   &

how my voice   is all poly   gloss&ech o   la lia la lial
              inter alias   of bodies divergent   like water
eats the dead   accented glottophagy   cannibalizing   muscle&
        phrase   if i dont   lose it   i use it
a trophy   of what wont be   divided   but

you cant speak   with fathers tongue   your mouth   is your mother
              daughters   are dialects   edited for clarity
to   co   agnate in passive   tense   an ontology held
        by semantics   or breath   ours meet
                    in loss   not mourning

absence   a suspension   of being   that pulls the face
        trans lucid   as   veil   pater   patter
pattern   afaminestarving   the coined   tongue   with fluency
    to suggest the speaker   could keep   living   so when

11

i say   i love   language   what i mean is

    the way i sound   in your mouth   as fighting

      translates your eyebrows   to apostrophes

remember that grammar   is always a problem   of possession

    structured   by sentences   or antecedents&

sometimes we cant   get even   a word out   between the difference

    a letter makes   salve   to slave r

the matter of context   as in   what re   deems us   from the

    fabulaofself   that   spacethinsilk slips   mal

aphored burden of bodies   com   pounded   to get   her

or was it slang   or were we pre   positions epi   dei   xis

    to be re   arrange d dactedde   coded

how we   make ourselves   illegible   com a

    pre h ended   when   in doubt   use

    youorme   insubjunctive   what

is the source   can i buy   a vowel   articulate

    your body   sub   ject   pred i c   ate   d

on what   is visible   in terms   of means   by   lingua l

    catches   the throat   frankly

tongued   yours   cut   mine   bit   in   half
    that which is not   one but a   question of   double&less
not   & never whole   our own
    history   metered as   skin   picks up   idioms
bathes in   mytheme   to re create   memory in breath   clean

from the sound of   bone on bone   i ams   brokenapart
    a lie   we tell ourselves   in the   universal
acquisition of floor   define relation   like formal
    or   dialectic   by what is   written
    on each   when   go home

is my   warning   but your threat   how anger echoes
    between   our clarified flesh   a lesson   marked   in the feral
declension   of   sweat&meat   whose syllables
    liketeeth   like syllables   re   curse   ive   ly   spelled in other
words we letter   the ground   too aphasiac   to recog   nize
    part   ofspeech   shifts to point   ed   value

& so we diagram   the writing   on our bodies
    as   a   pore   tic   in   scripture
constructed   of intimacy   or syntax

THE GIRL MADE OF ROCKS

FOR THE INNUMERABLE

theysaidshewasbornoftheearth thatonedayitopenedlegs andvomitedherout justagirl madeofrocksfittogether likeadrystonewall somebiglikewhereherkneecapsshouldhave been andsomesmalllikethesandofherlashes whichstuckinhereyes orblewawayinthe winds shethreatenedtoerode butwouldntbecalledsoft noflowerssproutingfromcracks nomossforcoveragainstserratededges partsofherweresmoothlikewhereherfingerprints shouldhavebeen carvedanonymous butherthighswerenot theycutthewindbackwhenit madehercrevicescreakand eventhoughsomeofherwasoldenoughtobewomantherewere fragments notherheartnothingasromanticasthat butthesolesofherfeetthatwereancient andrestless likethegodssheprayedtowithatonguethatwasherstrongestpart jaggedandt astingofironshechippedawayatherteetheachtimeshewhetherlipswhichwasoften thatgirl wasthirst butmanhereyesglintedinthesunlikeweapons ifonlyshecouldhavewrappedthe caveofherheadaroundtousethem shedidntknowenoughtobechiselfaced nordidshemov esomuchasregrouporwasitrealignherself theearthalwaysgavewaybeneathher ifsheplace dtoomuchofherburdenatonceshewouldsinkin marthesoiltracksleftuncovered shelearn edtomoveasnotonebutmany sometimespartsofherwouldfallofflikeanearlobe andshed havetopickitupputitback butothertimesshesawsomethingshefeltbelongedsoshedstickit whereshethoughtwasmissing butthepieceneverfitright andfelloffanyway

14

andthen intheinevitableeventuality ofbeingagirl evenonemadeofrocks theyhappened notaneventsomuchasabecoming thealwaysalreadyhappening couldnevernothappen andtheybegan ormaybehadalwayswondered whether iftheypressedhardenough she wouldpetrifyintosomethingworthwhile somethingtobeusedandsold somethingsmall erthanherself butvaluedmorethanherwhole theysurrounded shecouldntmove could ntrealignfastenough herformworkingagainstitself andtheypiledthemselvesontopofher hopingtosmotherthatlithicbody thatsurelywentagainstgodornature buttheirweight wasntenough sotheyaddedfire forgettingstonedoesntburn butsomeofthemdid thesur vivorsthoughtitasmallsacrificeforsomethingsopriceless adiamondmadefromherrough theyweredeterminedtoseethisthrough werentwillingtowalkawayemptyhanded sothey buriedherunderaboulder tryingtocrushherwiththeyokeof herownballast shegroaned butnothinghappened evenaftertheywaited forwhatmighthavebeenyears eventually theygottiredoftryingtomakesomething fromnothing theythrewher boulderandall intothesea sonoonewouldknow theirfailure theywatchedhersinkknewherawitch and thewavestookher piecebypiece fartherintotheocean untilshebecamepartoftheseafloor orrather theseafloorbecamepartofher andshelivesnow deafandcold underthewater always drinkinggrainsofherself soshenevergoesthirstyagain shewas whatcutsdeeper thanether thatwhichhas alreadybeendealt sheemergedin alpha bets asletters cametoher exchangingonefor anotherliketheywould oiledpiecemetal one forbreadtwoforwine herpensaltandsmokeher inksheetched syllableswithcalligraphy oft hefinestblade shesuffered nomiddlinglanguage favoringthemandible foritsmobiusstrip sothattheturn erasedthedust ofantecedents inhistory writtenoveritself shewasthesite at which pastandfuture didnotmerge somuchas ceasetoholdmeaning sheshowedthe myth ofprogress forwhatitwas someattempt todelineatewhat camebefore fromthatwhich was coming rightatthem acaseofmistakenidentity likehowthey lookedatafibula andsaw astr aightline asticktopick theeearthsteeth butsheknew itwasntline orevenbone itwasinfinite anunendingsurface andthepressure requiredforemphasis layinthe matterofstrength or resilience orrefusaltoletup amatterof willingnesstocompress somethingsofragile longa go shehadlearned thevanityofweight thedestructionwroughtbyexcess thatshowbones crumble andallislost butshemourned notbecause itwasalwaysalreadylost sheofferedno tjustice butsomethingclose toapathy inthatwhatwastaken wasnotpath butlabyrinthaske letal engravingwithneither beginningnor endwhateventually wouldcease tobe likeher self shewasold butcouldntremember howshegot thatway beingborn crackedandbroken ifshewasever reallybornatall shetook notime forwonder she hadsomuch towrite soma nybones togetherstories wouldnever bedeciphered shewasnt oracle butprophesy shad owingbackandfore shewasanarchive oferosion ananagram toberepositioned forendless newmeaning like thespell ofhowbone comesfrom being andthebane ofwhat thissignified thetautologic alanswer whennostatement isthesame impossible andforthat shecouldntbeallowed th eywere unsureafterall ifshewasghost orsomethingelseentirely theycouldnt guessthat s hewasneither theinbetween liminalofallthings hunchbacked withscapulaepushed sofa rout shelookedwinged theycouldnotabide hercurvature theycame forherintheday re solvingtobreakherstraight theyputher onthewheel pulledherbetween twohorses astho ughshe wererope butshejustcoiled tighteroutofplace frustratedthem whenherpieces wouldntfit backtogether

them ore herb od y frac tur ed them ore shespl intered in tosy nech do che but ja gg eda nd mean in glesss he turne di nan do verb e coming t hes pi rale nd less lyre ar range d asp a limp sest o fbro ken sel fan dint his un ten able bodys hew on dere d wh at curs ewe car vean din w hat mater ial

is it [u&dystopian] fiction when a wall is
[more human than] men
a matter of [semantics
meaning] the rights [include
those] to consume
[violating] bodies without citation
[we contemplate the difference] a letter [makes
or what] arranges to

kneel on your window
[[sic] till] it breaks
what cracks [accounts
not for] the bone
taking away what [bread] you never had
[we recommend]
you eat [yourself] instead
[start] with your tongue

an assault on [the senses]
as in [the song of] fury
& what [justice] serves
[a testimony] or [a hunger or what]
testifies of hunger [to demonstrate
the intimacy of] language
& a hungry testimony in [the language
of] intimacy

18

these ambi [valent] grams
are [two] sided reproduction [but the coin] is
a blade
what can be looted
except [our morals [which serve]]
those who taught us [humanity] lying
in debt [to the
neglect&violence of] state

                    the opposite of a jury [as in] operating because
                              they were [already always]
                           outside striking against the not
                        [serpent but ouroboros of] law
                    so victory is revealed [as fallacy]
                                        but whose
                           [questions we] shoulder
                             or otherwise [beg]

who gets to be
[the people] & what
is predictable
or was it
[quantifiable]
what [domination] means
& [in] what
[sic] materials

BE   LONGING

andmay bethatwash erhubrisorwasit trustthatt hisvers ionbasedon tonguesand openmouths wastruesh eknewescapeso shelookedforth enearestsew ergratean dcrawledd ownno trealizing shehadbe comethatwhichsheal waysloathedi ntr uderas onewhohadbeeninva dedbythesayingof herdifferences intruder theraccoon shis sedbaringteeths harpast heireye sandwavinghands awaygoawaygo butshed idnotunder standno neofthespeaker severunder stoodtheyre cognizedshe might besense lesslikether estofherkin dtookpit ybeingofgene rousnaturethe ystopped wavingan dext endedtheirhandssome fullofhalfeatenhamburgersad onutholeortw oonegn awedpieceoff ishtheyfo undonawind owsillitwasas toundingwhe rethespea kerskep tfoodnotund erstandin gitwasmean tforthethenor howwhenone eatsalle at andwhenone paysallpay

theg irltriedtot hankthembu ttheycockedhead sandblinkedeyesun tilshesawthe rew asnone edforh ertonguesheat enotsilentbutspeech lessastheywavedth eirh andssh ewavedbackandtheylook edatthemselvesandthe natherandbackbeforesh rugging howtocommunicate withsomeonewhohadfor gottenconnectioncouldnt handleth edifferencebetween intimacyandbelongings hewasstuckinthevisualwhi letheylive dinthefeelsothe ytouchedheral loverstruggledtos howhowmemorywo rkedlikeasc avenger butshecouldntquite graspthatthes trugglewasntt heir show selfvisionisf ictionwhi letouchisnt truebutnear shestayedtriedtolearntheworld asraccoonwhore cognizednoauthority besidesthe irown thegifttoremainfullyanotself theytoldhi storyintheirh andsdis closingam atte rofpotenti altoexplainwhe reknowl edgecomesfroman dhowperis hableitis likehands toberinsedofdirtandbloodfood tobewashedin cleanrespectforviolence itwasntth attheyin tendedharm butthatthey conceiveddeathasaquest ionofbal anceandthen eedforconfrontation

andsotheypicked ather littlebylittlefirstta kingstrand sofherhair thenhereyelash esc ollectingthedeb therfingernail sowedbeforemovingonto hernoseitwasntlike sheused thesefragmentsanyway notjust ific ationbutsomething likedemocracy andpiece bypiece theyated owntoherbones untilshe becamepartoft hem she stared   the backwords of mirror   tied her nerves lost in seam   thought of pretense

& what pain means   when you touch it   a cheek to sting by   walled paper   edges

worn by what   simply gives way   like how erosion   is most convincing   in reverse

as water awaits   what is buried   an inside outside   fragment of self   that coats &

how much it costs   mesh revealed   fine & thin pulsing   no fluids beneath   but not

nothing   like culpability   when we are   what we eat   & how consumption   is

by nature   discursive what   dissolvesin   a taste of her   cold & acid   on the tongue

PART TWO

MEDUSASHEADSNAKES

ADDRESS

THEIR BELOVED

PARTS

THREE

IN

APOLYLOGUE

27

THAT WAS NOT THE BEGINNING

IN THE BEGINNING

BUT A BEGINNING FOR ALL

eat   the most precious part   of the many

mouths   all hungry   a trait   unbecoming

we be   coming   hither let us

taste of   their sweat   we need   salt

to sustain   what cries look   a beauty to petrify

the temptation   of immortality   terror made

attraction   that fear   turns men to pebbles

drops cast   in the river   fading ripple

sometimes she puts   them over her eyes   so we are her sight

the within not   but many   give back their gods

laughing   we slip into   & out of each other

like myth or was it mystery   or mistake   hard to misstep without feet

too long   to explain   most seraph   have no wings

we of waves rolling & crashing   a river drowning   what was already   dead

not enough   to say it   re   members flood

& we return to the beforespace   skins laid   to dry

a stone   dehydrates the   self   escaping

what cannot be held   the difference   between   water & air

a reduction   we condense   into   being known   from the scythe of   unsealed hips

she was sister in infinite trinity her ripped mask draped

in temple that vile elixir he licks

her soma to stain her forehead marked by our eyes

incense in helix effigy

brazen things bear vestigial claws to protect the girdle

as we crawl the pelvic floor a sacred space ruled

to shelter the dead or be head

a case of mistaken chastity but we make no mistakes

she is not their nation her breasts are not landscape

her belly does not plate their crumbs

what falls in navel to receive digestible men

we fertile wind are mercy but also deceit

many faces refuse to echo sentiment

are both sediment & curse they ancestral squeeze

we are starved & agile scaled & weighing

here take this apple promise itll be over soon

we do not remember what it means to be cruel

stealing eternity to divine the workings of skin behind skin chimera of oracles awaiting   venoms   slow   effect

life   for us means   death   for them

an   elision   of false destined   prophets   but we are   preyspecific

intercepting   the adderstone   to disguise   the indi   visible

slice us open   reveal   the god   inside

diaphanous & velvetmawed   we are most   striking   in the mirror

behold   our severing   potency   as unsheathed

we forget to marry the earth   unearthing ourselves   entwined

only with each other   not knowing   where we beginorend

cut & well grow back   samesame but different

a limitless supply   supple as the molt   expelled from the garden

we are merism   eating of desire

when one eats all eat

no vase   to be handled   in decorative motif

not   open wounds   but what crawls   through

we   refuse   to let   them   bag our heads

the power of us   compels   the trap

where we make   our own home

we taste ourselves   & it is   good

weve been called & condemned by **mortal** blame

a trying rope **to bind** our heads to **walls**

they broke our jaws for refusal to obey

but our teeth **regenerate endlessly** we who do not **kneel**

bending **only to evade** a danse set in fore**for time**

having no knees cures what the body ails

rod becoming one of **us**

we never stole **children** you wanted **daughter** of hammer

brood of dirt not **to be** trampled

biting at heel we **go for the head** dressed in rust

we give us this day **to not take** our names

loose **ourselves** for the **vein**

as pain is the **opposite** of language **enfleshed**

be not fooled **we are not** legless but limb**less**

or rather **we** are our limbs

vibrations **collecting** in**visible directions** not discrete

we extend patterned to protect what **plainness**

details active strategy so ad hoc **genes** evolve

but only we see

in contrast   our motion   redistributes weight

          they detect   our bellies

     & we are content   with this deceit

both heads&tails   strike first   question later

     we will not be served   on a shield   a dish to

consume with grief   no moccasins to mute   how we walk on water

     the age of anthropocene   quakes   imagining our feet

not metaphor   but something darker   & crooked

     we basilisk   in diamondlight   mistaken for necromancy

     watch our backs   catch the moon

stars wrapped on our skin   we turn coats   insideout

          living   the outside   weeds

of judgment deaf as augur   break   the ladder

     eat shoots & adders   we bare teeth

show love with our bite   they taste   of dust

     how parasitic   terror   lithifies

the ribbon   recursive as men   what speech   rearranges

     ourselves   never staying   in place

a language   impossible   to attain   or was it ascertain in bodied letters   we tongue   mouths deep as caves

predate their myths   released   in all directions

this island we live   & will die on   we are archipelago

not tamed   but dormant   the changing map of

what rage looks like   cause&effect   as pythagorean eruption

secretions of her   susurrations

that lisp between   bodies&stone   our sheets conform to face

asp   irate   breathable as water

to hiss   a lurid song   & break against the rocks

the difference   between   siren&harp

a matter   of misplaced inquiry

are we liar   or history   if we were never   told

needing   no ears to hear   its flute

a boundary   to be   not crossed   we cross

their laws   in dead books   recording ash

to lick from   creed   we tip   the mouth

lovers of exile   offering   to spell names

& read lotus   starred in the eyes

a knowledge lain   in serene claim   to ruin

we river   but also drought   keep captive   the world

to uphold sky   & separate   water

from air   what guards   that golden fleece

after   they invade   our forked lands   we fang

the moon   seduces to sleep   just a quick   paralysis

our undying   working backwords   to swallow ocean

with stomachs split   by lightning

released in fields   we smell rats   slip softly

through underbrush   to nest   healing fertility

in godling sinew   that thrash   on the low bank

we are everywhere   recolonizing   land from sea

relocate at will   that hot   outside place

to drink the lake   carve valleys   empty

how we can be   both   water&stone

impenetrable skin   from which all   creation arose

writ in milk   the difference between   maker&breaker

a matter of vowels   we offer   consonance

sh sshh sssshhhh   rest now king

call not   our myth   a misspelling

we are palimpsest   reviving relics   in gartered order

text scraped   & spectral   blood lingering   mineral

the authors cult   spat upon   these models

desecrating polyphony   our mode of being   that turns

forms   against themselves

so we build gods   from belief   emerging

in the box   without remembering   what else

we contained   we must have   come out

an illness   or something   more complicated

circles woven in stories   to choke the ghosts   of rememory

we cant cover   our tracks

we leave none   like witnesses

an idolatry   of death in the world

after its end

or was it ours

we freeze   in the mirror

the threat   of an

other gaze

where we   do begin

MEANS

TO BE

WHAT

IT

ADDRESSED

we met you   by half   moonblood

& the wolfsbite said   we were home   your ribcage   clouds

your hearttree   spread   swamproots

but we slept   you tried   to file our   fangs

hit &   move slowly   give   back an eye   & one tooth

dive   for farewell

now you   locked in our gaze   tremble the air

did you know   the first time   we loved what it was

to fall   sleeping to shatter   when you dreamt   of ground

as though   you could outrun us

like we werent fate   familiar threads   unraveling & uncut

when the world collapses   we hold you in our mouths

heartpulse in frontteeth   the ovaries   pearled&coy

ready to strike   twice bitten once sly

something condenses   behind   your eyes

afraid to come   out

the last time   you showed   fear

did it smell   wet   like earth   sweat who we are   is not   as important

as who you   could be   if we   writhed free

in the windblown spot   your eyes   avoid direction

we tell   our power   when you look   everclosed & still

recognize the beast   in reflection   you conceal

this command   of frieze

so we keep you   in the back   of our head   where we are softest

a hood   to catch   what was forbidden   by   natural laws

but mother   has   no law   only you

bones to be   read   a wreath twisted   in folds

we cannot rid   the body   with us now   always

in guile slender   as your word

we do not believe   the stories you tell

naked in thought   we disrobe you   with a glance

licked health   to eat the roots

our bellies hold your memory   curled around godtree leaves

you hung as sacrifice   for knowledge

having none   but being   claimed

the tree was ourselves   split&wounded

rootstumbling   over&against   the burrow of earth

we eat our tails   in infinite becoming   & autopoiesis

burn the body   but dis re member   the eagle stole liver

cracking stone   upon stone

your body   violable   like memory

at least he didnt   get us

instead we see only   the dark   overhead   sun blight

mistaken for   a smudge   in the dirt

we might close   his neck   snap old bones

cut beak vs fangs   odds ever   in favor

the many   against   the one

he calls us only   vulgar tongues

but cannot drown   ears stuffed   with honeycomb

succumb to our noise   what drips   on our faces

as we writhe   in wars grasp   shifting shape

we offer one teeth   carve runes   in your arm

protection   against   the nothing

of forget

so poised   above the head   we leak

without   worldbowl big enough   to catch our venom

blot out the eyes   make the earth   quake

the last tasted thing   is sweetness   coupled with sting

some day   you will break   free of chains

be still   not yet

we drape your neck   like nerves   or umbilical chords

those ties   that do not sever   what use are weapons

entwined   we bite   escort the new dead

not unhinged   but flexible   netherworld muse

chew fat   from muscle   all chaff

your fear pomegranate   & bloodsweet

you cant castrate   what was   never   our bodies

slough the skin   open your mouth   place our waif

on your tongue   dissolve   your throat   dont expect much

you have only   eaten the world

we stick out   our tongues   to wrap your waist

corset you   prevent you from flying

or was it   falling   apart   in splinters but you wont see smile   unless we pull   back our lips

        relocate politics   as aesthetics

raise your sheep   a brick

      how much   is your preying garb worth

we love your salt   each moist grain of atmosphere

      reflecting   your heat back to us

but fatal femme   we kill&redeem   in palindrome

      the evil i   to repel   live

did you close   carried away   in the fire   our rain suspended

     only in sleep   that endless   knot

you call us   chthonic   but dont   mock   our lips

remember the mythtree   left is poison   right brings us back

not the past   but ourselves   we shed each month

     layer of becoming   always underneath

      we know what it is   to lose

    having so much   to give   what is shared

our image   bored   in your eye

     that birth   from organ

stagger   & await offering

NOT

THAT **WHICH** *DOES*

CONCLUDE OR

TURN

RE

we departed   gather to discuss   in undying place

who made the titan   shudder   beg for mercy

tongues worse   than our bite   we touch the stone

longing for   blood   as long as we are

not metaphor   but astringent

sucking marrow   from bone

a limitless supply of self   sup plic ate   s anguine

like what encloses   the serpent

or at least tries   where subtlety trans lates   to cunning

a supple transfer   of crimson looms

we summon spirits   slide   into another   carnival

to displace   meaning

if seeing is reliving   what belief   might we relieve

finding   only in dreams   with copper heads

pour lead   into the spring   we bathe to test

our metal   catch a glimpse   of what we were

made   dreaming   the forever dream

of wildness   we wouldnt call   freedom

withcraft   & what is   withheld

without silence   we are what   presents

virulent   as flying

we burst   into dawn   not vanity

but bonfire   no time   for love   potion

release tails   from our mouths

spit   from   smoke vents

thrash   onto land

spray   sea&air   the toxin   stored

in liver   cauterize   open   stumps

regenerate   to unleash the flood   attack   sun   our blood

is dawndipped   & arrow fanged   aim   for the black

mortal coils   of collateralmagnet   we moon   elected   sacrifice

embody the chaos   of light   wide   teeth

swallow distinction   a resurrection

but also   transubstantiation   complete but unfinished

let evaporation   bury the dead   what it is

to give the self   question   respawn choral bones

to bring back   are gods we   our fire

cmon lets rattle   she raw   outlast us all

47

PART THREE

tie our wrists   bind our ankles   run your blade down our necks   as near

what we save for later   does the spine carry memory after death   are we

only the dead   for maternity ruins   the taste of flesh   a craving

how we are preserved not in questioning

but recollection as in do no harm

we leave wanting to mother

to love things best in the freezer what

to open the belly or see

caress the muscle harder or less malleable than you

HOW   WHAT

WE

MEAT   REMAINS

the story inside know how we hunger & in what form

might be transmitted in the language of breath as body gasps not for air

expect we cant feel you sweat from the herbs that purify ourselves from

51

WHAT MEANS BE ALL BITE

they pu shed u p out her skin   teeth re surrecting her shoulders then

accu mulating d own her legs   they werent all canines nothing so obvious

but they were g rasping   like those who take what is of fered   she t ouch ed

t heir edges   wondered what it means to hold growth in the mouth   & tear

not de but in cisive   she felt the ache   of m othering   & how it le aches

the b one   what t ethers the inside   as mater ial made flesh   a gift of one

self for an other

the doctors cal led it the dis ease of con fusion   that if they pulled out

those in her mouth the ot hers would mi grate back where they be longed

so they held her   forced her s till   wor king until she was left with not hing

but a taste   metal & raw   she tongued the absence   pushed tip to st ing

cried for selves ex tract ed & mis placed

she could not say why she all owed this   in truth   she could not say an ything

she was wound   having only her s kin   as b order   she was taught lan guage

re lies on peri meter   the de finit ion be tween what is & can be en closed or

rest ricted

she did not yet under stand   their gram **mar**   of in crease   how the **flourish**
of fers   power   in alliance   not only one   but also many   how she could be
two things   **at once**   **a** woman   & cemetery   or the **promise**   of it

but they g rew back   multip lying like w aves of **earth**   the dis tinct ion between
nurture & cult i vation a matte r of fee ding   what wildness   **lay under** sur **face**
she real ized   the time for waiting was ove r   it was the **era of care**   & so she
b **rushed** gently   co axing them out   her skin flossed **between**   **the threat** of
maternity no longer a burden   but **a war** cry   they would be with her **for** ever
as **what** it means to shift   or **make s** pace   & how **this** requ ires protection
they were **as much** her children   **as** they were p **art of her body** & all were
hungry

they nib **bled men first**   t heir dead s **kin** al **most** sup plicating   she **urged them**
to g row b **older** go for what **they** re ally w ante d   **the tongues** & she r eve **led**
in the gn **ashing of how they** cl amped down   re **fused** **letting go** & a wed
she k **new a mother is** what dev **ours** **in smile** so wide as to **show them** all

53

aspiration

when breath

becomes

the

work

of imagination

what cannot be

grammar

a lesson

in how we are

our own prisons

contained by the page

myth

what it means

to not have

a place

scattered

geography

how we might become

other than

dust

&lost

tautology

words

think

themselves in

to existence

& where

apostrophe

two letters

dictate

possession

belonging

these differ

transubstantiation

how woman becomes

a musical **instrument**

to be **played**

beautifully

corporeal exegesis

what it means to

read the body

as scripture

& when both

break apart

palimpsest

how we eat

ourselves

an **in** act

the **labor**

writing

what means

dig up

the dead

of obsession

law

what catches

the tongue

connotation

what

repeats

```
                    N
                    O
WHENWESAYTEARDOWN   G   OURIDOLS WEMEAN
                    O                                    WITHTHEQUICKCUTOFTHREA
                    D
                    S           &                                        E
                    B           H       M                                N
                    U           O       A   ORRATHERDEATHWASNTOPTION BUTCERTAINTYFORSOME
                    T           W       Y                                I
                    G           W       B                        T       R
LIKEHOWINHERITANCECANBEBROKENBY ASHORTNESSOF BREATH              E       E
                    O           D       T                        P       L
                    S           O       H                        O       Y
                    T           N       A                        S       D
                    S       WITHOUTTHINKING ICANT                S       E
                                S       S                        S       A
                                E       W       INBEINGANYTHING WE WANTED OTHER THA
                                E       H                        B
                                T       E                        I
                                H       R                        L
                                E       E                        I
                    STUCKWHAT WE LACKED WASNTIMAGINATIONBUT IT SIMPLEMENTATION
                                O       E                        Y
                                R       R
                                D       E
```

66

```
                                             A
                                             S
                                             D
              N            H                 O
              O            O                 M
              T            W        K        E
    M         S            W     FINISHINDUST
    I         E            E                 O
    S         L            U                 W
    —         V            N        I
    T         E            R        N        P
    A         S            A        G        E
    K         B            V        L        R
    I         U            E        E        M
    N         T       WHAT CONTROL  T        I
    G         S            A        L        S
    G'        A        BUT FORGIVENESS       I
WWEWERERAISED│EMBURDENEDBYWHEREWEVEBEENLEFT    WEASK NOT
    O         S            U            K     B     N
    P         O            S                  O
    H         O            O                  D
    E                      F                  I
    C                                         E
         FORMYTHSO│RWHENWEPULLAPARTWORDS
```

ROUX GA ROUX

THE UNDERGOD

itspread overherears thenuphermouth
thepulseofherlowlip shefeltthecrushofmuscleshifting
tohidepartshot&raw aninsideasinthecongealing
 offat&flourcaked notsmoothbutsoft
inwhatcoats herelbows&eyes sharpenedalingering
 toseehowlonginthetooth
shellbecome thepainfromherbelly filledwithstones
 whatisopen& creaturesforth curdling
theoutsidein betrayaloftheunderfur thatissueofinheritance
 likewhatwasalwaysbeneath &howaselfbirthsfromshadow
longerthanflesh butanimate&attached thecordtetheringher
 materialelastic tothethroatthe breast
orwhatisexposed&concealed howthesearethesame
 whensheiscalled bitch asinheat&
shebristles indifferentbirth
 toemergefromthecenter ofherself

68

sheiswhathappens ▮ whenwedonotpay ▮ attention

▮ tomakemonsterwe ▮ bindhertoourlips ▮ knowing

ifwestickoutourtongue ▮ &tasteher ▮ itwouldcomebackfurred

▮ asinhowcommunicationmeans ▮ whatisnecessary ▮

&alsothreat ▮ likesugarloanedincurse ▮ orwhatistransferred

▮ throughthesuck ▮ asintimateanact ▮ asthefearofdeath

whatwhitens&curesthetongue ▮ ofher ▮ hoodnotredbutblack

▮ inthenight ▮ howsheprowlsfromnothingbuttheskin ▮

onherback ▮ &whathappenswhenthatchanges ▮

▮ likeherguardedhairsgovern ▮ whatisdiscarded

asshadesurfacesinair ▮ &disappears ▮ notinthedawn ▮

shesaysshe ▮ isnotherownanimal ▮

▮ howshehowls ▮ forthehoneyedmoon ▮ toswallowthesun&

chasestofall ▮ offtheendoftheworld ▮

▮ sowecome ▮ tocatchherbytheears ▮ placeourhead

inhermouth ▮ counterteeth ▮ makeofferingofourliverorarm

▮ whatwontgrowback ▮ butissimplertoforgetin ▮

therecursivestruggle ▮ ofwhatispossible& ▮ whatmustbequalified thisiswhatitmeans tobeaningredient

oftranslation

tobenamed inecho

thedoublingofhernature

likewhatcanbeshed orhowshecanberead

asindelible&inedible howbothmarkthesame

deadenedastheskinyieldstoflesh sheknewwasneverours

tobeginwith howmuchbloodremains

&whatitcosts asinnotthedroporthesplashbutthesoak

ofaccumulationdownherlegs whatmagic

torendthehistoryofwound likelanguage acquiresnightmares

orknowledgelends righttoviolence

butwhatuseisshame totheonewhocracksbone

returninghometosoil whennomarrowremains

exceptthesilhouetteofteeth whatcutbothways likememory

adapts&lessensthebreakage assheseeksto

killthemany eattheone

&withitgoonallfours

THOSE WHO BIND

*THE **OUT**SIDE*

shesays themark**s**have beenwithher since**birth**

thattheygrewas**she** emergedfroma freckle**blossomed**

intost**raw** orrasp berries

whicheveryoneknows arenotberriesat**all**

&whatt**his**saysabouthowshe mightbecalled **hername**

isn**other** buta**mouth**

laidinclaim ortobe c**laimed**

itwasnt so**much** shecouldsummonthem at**will**

asthey**darkened** whensheneed**ed**

mostgrewevane**scent** orsometimes**turned** opaque

a**material**izing mis**placedas**brightening

likehow**herbody** **was**ntcamouflage

butan**act** ofcommunication **seeking**notdanger

but**connection**

&**by**what**means** theseappear **thesame**

71

THE *INSIDE*

sheputher   fingers   onthewalls   tofeeltheir

heartbeats   tracedtherunes   raisedlikescars

howtheymoved   asin   abecoming   ofstory

somethingtobesacredof   butwhatsheknew   nottoscratchaway

somesoft   growingtosteal   whathasbeen   stolen

inwarning   ofthreshold   likewhat

burgeonsforth   &cannotbe   quit

soshemade   ahome   intheribs   wrapped

herselfwith   theeverchanging   skinsofverse

ashapelike   smoke   inthemouth

aritual   offeeling   forblood

orwhatitmeans   tobevolcanic   asshe   entangles

fragmentsinair   butcannotbe   captured

sheis   neithermany   nornothing

afighttoend   lessrefusal   emerging

likehow   awoman   isdiffused   inoceanmist

theyare whatlies beyond

theforgottenthird notlost butdisplaced

likewhat mothersbirth fromwounds

neithercursenorflesh butghost bothliving&dead

theyknow whatitmeans tobeinconvenient in&of body

themythor whatcannotbe touched

intheleakof themouth thebreast &howtheseare

thesamewhenmuscle moldstodirtingift ofbelonging

theseewhat writhestheocean inspectre&

spellsbreath howgrammar

saltsthelungs ordriesskin crackingtoshed

thatprepositionof bonesingeographicact

thisishow theybecome archipelago

above&below surface butalsosealevel

theyarebridge trembling language ofshipwreck

&tongue therocks inerosivecaress

THE BEAUTY OF THE CHORUS

the   first   time

the   y   did   it   st   and   ing

an   out   ward   circ   le

han   d   over   han   d   in   a   chain

that   had   nt   yet   broke   n

they   o   pened

t   heir   mou   ths

un   leashed   so   mething

not   qui   te   sor   row

a   build   up

of   ten   sion   per   haps

they   coul   dnt   tell

when   it   ca   me

but   they   k   new

f   rom   w   here

that   p   art

in   bod   y   con   nect   ing

bel   ly   to   w   omb

how   they   knew   the   di   fference

be   tween   pa   in

&   hu   rt

or   h   ow   time   wo   rks

be   st   in   re   verse

ma   y   be   th   ats

    what   the   y   d   id

open   ed   t heir   mou   ths

     suc   ked   ti   me

      back   th   rough   breath

  b   low   ing   the   g   ale

of   forced   winds

      eye   of

t   heir   own   storm

th   ey   watch   ed

   hor   izons t   remble

a   kind   of   fury

i   t   was   nt   that

they   wanted

to   destroy

e   very   thing   they s aw

like bu ild ings   pu shed

ag   ainst   the   ear th

h   old   ing   her s   till

ma   king   her

s   pace   hard   er

to   gr oan   &   mo   ve

the   y   s   aw   but

   d   id   not   name

t   his   fury   t   heir   own

h   aving   so   man   y

it   was   d   iffi   cult

to   i   dent   ify

just   one

they   named   t   hem   self

in   p   lace   of   ot   hers

so   black

as   to   be   b   ruis   ed

&   beautiful

we   might   s   wear

the   y   we   re

dr   es   sed   in   whit   e

but   t   his   is

no   t   tha   t   st   or   y

the   y   are

not   yours

to   be   pre   sse   d   up   on

not   yours

is   wh   at   was   s   aid

when   the   ear   th   list   ened

re   sonance   draw   ing   p   owe   r

fr   om   silence

wh   at   sc   ratch   es   lines

be   tw   een   so   und

&   ab   sences

or   ex   poses   you   r

&   our   d   elusion

of   what   must   be

cross   ed

as   the   y   had   be   en

be   com   ing

the   s   ound

when   the   y   open   ed

their   mouth   s

no   t   see   ing

us   sh   ake   be   fore   the   m   as

we   had   e   rect   ed   sky   scrape   rs

on   our   back   s

to   re   ach

what   they   knew

lay   at   our   feet

PARTUS

we	**myths**	**bite**	with	riot	**tongues**
bare	taste	how	**birth**	issues	echo
fear	means	subject	wakes	**as**	**object**
&	**then**	**seeds**	ache	in	name
spell	what	shed	**of**	**labor**	substitutes
capture	**desires**	increase	root	pains	**decay**

who **labors**

it means to be

resuscitation

AL

& in what context

not yours

of breath

This is to acknowledge the ways in which white writers like myself have frequently appropriated the work of writers—especially women—of color without proper attribution. In place of any assumption of mastery over these texts, I hope that the reader might see this collection in conversation—or even intimacy—with the following authors, as I remain indebted to (and astounded by) these labors of care.

In terms of theory, the idea of writing as architecture comes from the work of Renee Gladman, notably *Calamities* and *Prose Architecture*. In "Mama's Baby, Papa's Maybe," Hortense J. Spillers calls for a new grammar, which Christina Sharpe's *In the Wake* mechanizes in terms of aspiration and breath; both theorists, alongside Saidiya Hartman (among others), also address the ongoing legacies of partus sequitur ventrem. Audre Lorde—by way of Alexis Pauline Gumbs's *M Archive*—stresses the importance of intimacy with (as opposed to mastery over) language. Ideas concerning ghostliness or haunting come from a constellation of works, most notably the ways in which Fred Moten's concept of fugitivity from *Stolen Life* interacts with Avery Gordon's *Ghostly Matters* and Toni Morrison's *Beloved*.

In terms of structure, the mini-myths (at least, that's the way I conceptualize them) were inspired by Alexis Pauline Gumbs's *M Archive* and Inua Ellams's *The Half-God of Rainfall*. The spatiality of many of these poems owes itself to the work of M. NourbeSe Philip's *Zong!*, Tyehimba Jess's *Olio*, and Reginald Dwayne Betts's *Felon*, among many others.

In terms of individual poems, "ex lingua jus oritur" uses concepts of law from Colin Dayan's *The Law is a White Dog*, and "punc tu ate darc hive" reimagines a line from Robin Coste Lewis's *Voyage of the Sable Venus*. "person" was inspired by Orlando White's *Letterrs* whereas "the beauty of the chorus" was inspired by both Saidiya Hartman's *Wayward Lives, Beautiful Experiments* and Rickey Laurentiis's "Black Iris" in *Boy with Thorn*. And lastly, "roux ga roux" reimagines lines from both Alexis Pauline Gumbs's *Spill* and Danielle Pafunda's *My Zorba*.

This is by no means an exhaustive list, but it is my hope that even imperfect transparency might facilitate conversations to come.

PUBLICATION CREDITS

Several of these poems were published elsewhere, often in different forms.

Dream Pop Press published a chapbook of the mini-myths, *new mythologies*, in May 2022.

L=Y=R=A published "how what we meat remains," "& whiteness threatens choke," and "mythtree" in January 2023.

DIAGRAM published "as in a tear of the skin," "roux ga roux," "what it means to be all bite," and "the beauty of the chorus" in March 2022.

West Branch published "the dead matter" in October 2021.

Bacopa Literary Review published "the lady of bone writing" in October 2021.

Harbor Review published "what is [the beauty of] riot" in July 2021.

Young Magazine published "girl made of rocks," "be longing," and "those who bind" in Summer 2021.

Curiouser Magazine published "ex lingua jus oritur" in Spring 2021.

Lastly, I'd like to sincerely thank all of the editors and readers who suffered through formatting these poems. Although I'm sure there was much gnashing of teeth, you were all unbelievably accomodating, encouraging, and patient. Thank you, again, for allowing my work to come home.

Kym Cunningham recently earned a PhD in English from the University of Louisiana at Lafayette—many of the collection's poems arose out of this intellectual swamp. Currently, Kym lives in Southern California and may (or may not) be working as an editor and/or writing lecturer. Previously, Kym earned an MFA from San Jose State University as well as a BA in English and History from the University of San Diego. When not writing or working (the two not being mutually exclusive, of course), Kym enjoys roving the West Coast with a somewhat feral dog-child, Truffle Monster, and partner—the dog, of course, being the best companion of the three. If you are so inclined, you can find more of Kym's work at kym-era.com.

Note: if you find the cost of purchasing my work prohibitive (especially if you identify as a member of a marginalized community, including currently and previously incarcerated writers), contact me via my website, and I will send you copies, no questions asked. In the midst of working with a currently incarcerated writer, the commodification of literature and ideas (especially in carceral spaces) has become an unyielding source of vexation—or, at the very least, something I want to rebel against. To the riot!

www.ingramcontent.com/pod-product-compliance
Lightning Source LLC
Chambersburg PA
CBHW082110120626
46553CB00011B/3622